When All Is After

poems by

Peter Barton

Finishing Line Press
Georgetown, Kentucky

When All Is After

Dedicated to my father, Bernard,
who loved language and could recite oceans of poetry from memory.
He tried to sing away his wounds—mostly sea chanties.
But they are a precious part of my inheritance.

Copyright © 2023 by Peter Barton
ISBN 979-8-88838-258-5 First Edition
All rights reserved under International and Pan-American Copyright Conventions. No part of this book may be reproduced in any manner whatsoever without written permission from the publisher, except in the case of brief quotations embodied in critical articles and reviews.

ACKNOWLEDGMENTS

This book was shepherded along by Julia Bailen with help from Ella Harmon and my inspiring wife, Jane Startz. Special thanks to poet Annie Thomas and to my daughter, Kate Barton. Thank you to the Westmoreland Arts & Heritage Festival for publishing "My Father Is in My Closet" and "When All Is After" as the second and third prize winners of their 2021 Poetry & Short Story Contest. I must also thank The Orchard Street Press for including "Rug Ride" and "My Father Is in My Closet" in their 2021 issue of *Quiet Diamonds*. And, of course, thank you to Finishing Line Press for publishing this book.

Publisher: Leah Huete de Maines
Editor: Christen Kincaid
Cover Photo: "Boboli Gardens, Florence" by Peter Barton
Author Photo: Jane Startz
Cover Design: Elizabeth Maines McCleavy

Order online: www.finishinglinepress.com
also available on amazon.com

Author inquiries and mail orders:
Finishing Line Press
PO Box 1626
Georgetown, Kentucky 40324
USA

Table of Contents

Rug Ride 1

When All Is After 3

On the Sands of the Sidewalk 4

My Father is in My Closet 6

Your Side of the Bed 7

Dip of No Return 8

The Granpa Diaries 9

Backing Up Today 12

Step Away from the House 14

Mike Rows On… 16

"Diving for the Sun" photo by Peter Barton 18

Startle Reaction 19

Veterans' Benefits 21

A Phone is Ringing in the Next Room 22

Bruises 23

He Had Always Lived a Laptop Life 24

There Is Coming to You and Going Away 26

"Reaching for Sky" photo by Peter Barton 27

Days of Holding On 28

Blessed Are the Joys 30

We'll Go on One Ticket 31

I Will Keep House for You 32

She Waits Patiently for Me 34

Rug Ride

A wet Saturday night
And the girls can't decide
To go uncool with umbrellas
Or risk their curls without.
The street sways free
Looking for a fight
Late for a connection…

No prowling tonight.
Not for me.
With you, sweet boy
I'm always where I want to be.

We are taken by the give
Of our dusky rug
The amnesty of the evening
Heals up our headlines.

I stroke your forehead
As my father stroked mine
Though never long,
Never long
Enough…

And I realize how much
Through all my life
I've expected what I gave
To come back to me.

But all I got
Was a chance at the end
To stroke my dad's hair
As he lay dying.

It took us that long
To turn all the tables.

So
I stopped waiting for boomerangs
Of such unwrinkled joy
Giving doesn't mean
You get.

We don't breathe as one
You are twice as fast
Muffled in my armpit
Your hair so fine
It sticks to my chin
Reminds me to shave.

I have you now
So close to my life
That it seems very near
When you'll stroke my hair
As I stroked my father's
On that dry rainy night
When the walls drew in.

When All Is After

When all the greenery is gone
And the wind that kept us tossing
Has died in the grass by the river
You will be laughing still,
I know.
Chin tucked madly
Against your chest.
And for your midnight reminiscences
A toilet seat kept warm
For your sighs and singing.

I will still be waiting
In the long echoing hall
Leaning my grateful shadow
Against the grinning wall.
And as you roll home
My dreams will track you
Down side streets, cackling
While swallows call and streetcars clang
And the little cracks in the dawn
Fly off singing.

On the Sands of the Sidewalk

I seem to be stories now
Stories repeated
Rehearsed, condensed
Burps of easy laughter
At myself
Creaks and cricks and rumblings
Fear of the stairs
And bending down
And flapping my wings
In yoga class.

Delicious suspense each time
I retrieve a rag of memory
Hearing its rumble
As it comes caroming down the chute
A ball under the bowling alley
Popping up to croaked applause
From the back of my head

I watch a… *much* older man
Stranded in shuffles
On the tilting sands of the sidewalk.
Flotsam? Jetsam?
The ambulance will decide.

Says hello
To everyone he doesn't know
And will never remember.

A tear?
Just the cold.

Where did his tomorrows go?
Stolen?
Or too few to count.

The bus comes.
He lets it leave.

A question rises in his throat.
A shadow passes.

He raises not his worthless eye
But his ear.

In a blink
The sidewalk tilts back.
Throws him toward the curb.

Will it ever
Come back to him
About this tree
Across the park
The one his daughter
Kept trying to climb
Until she lost interest.
He just loves the mournful wave
Of those slim, slim branches
Sort of the way his wife danced
When she stopped wanting to murder him

There's the mailbox
He used to thump
Then lift his daughter
High onto
And let her slide
Til her shriek caused him shame
So he thumped it again
Growling punishment at it
Then she hugged it
In forgiveness
And they both walked home wondering
Who would get
Those chummy letters inside.

While across the street
I wonder
When the moon will be getting up tonight
And whether the days are getting longer
While mine are getting shorter
And wondering where wonder went
When
With a slap,
it returns.

My Father Is In My Closet

My father is in my closet
His smell, hanging way back,
Bent over in the dark

I remember a yellow plaid
In our old house
He didn't feel the need
To toss 'em in the laundry
So his shirts ripened
Overwhelmed the mothballs
Shuddered a bit
When I checked on them
As if they felt
A subway trembling past

And I thought I felt him
Put a hand on his own shoulder
When illness visited
And the stale air stirred
And his shoes reshuffled
And my mother's perfume
Seemed so very far away
And the winds breathed sadly
And the sky failed
To lean in
To stroke his forehead…

Your Side of the Bed

I don't sleep on your side of the bed.
It's drowsy there, unrumpled.
I won't even kick it.
The wind stays away, too.
I smooth the sheet tenderly
And make sure not to smell
Whatever breathes out
When the covers billow.

The night isn't deep enough
The moon's hot and cold.
I get up and skate the dark
Wanting whispering corners
Swept into their shadows.
No clock strikes
But the windows rattle out Winter
And the snakes slither out
Curling round my ankles
As I begin to shimmy-shake
And dance the dawn away.

Dip of No Return

Half a breast stroke
Into our closet
I pause to sniff.
The tide laps my ankles
I think I'm breathing Now
But I'm really drifting
Skimming the pond
Going so far back
Beyond the first morning
When I took your sweater off
Past the last time
You hung that lacy bra
On the wrong door knob.
Until a sheet of seafoam
Laps at our blotchy shins
And we are floating behind
Newer days
Older mornings
Scrubbing the lemony sun
Off the faded rug
Breathing afternoons so tangled
In the ripe bedclothes
That you turned away
And didn't bother
To promise to come back…

The Granpa Diaries

Why is no one awake yet?
Don't they want to see the sun get a leg up
Over those witch-haired winter trees?

True they don't have my dog
The one who died in '93
To lick their faces,
Get them up early
To make some mischief.

Excuse me, quiet house.
I have to yell at my newspaper.
Then yawn a few large
And clear my throat
So I can yell at the tv.

You see
I'm a hard-charging
Score-settling
Endangered species.
Take a step closer
You'll get your assumptions
Braised.

A noise upstairs.
Am I due for a scolding?
Not today.

His Mom lets grandson David scamper
Down the stairs into my arms
To save the Universe.
We sharpen our light-sabers
While I wipe his nose.
Flushed with the prospect
Of kicking imaginary ass.

We hug.
We High-Five.
I will never forget this tender moment…

Except I know I will.
This very afternoon.

After a lot of yelling, parry and thrust
The enemies retreat
And we breathe easy,
Pat our own backs…

He lays his tousled head
On my bony chest
And I realize that after all
He doesn't fear me
The way he used to.

There was a time
 I tried to teach him
To use the remote
Because "One day…"
I choked out a whisper
"One day I won't be here
To find Sillyface Boobah for you."
A pause.
Did he understand?
He then gave me
The Look.
A "get back in your hole"
Kind of look.
And I resolved right then
To stop looking ahead.

Today he finds a book
And before Once Upon A Time
Gets to Twice
His breath slows
His eyes close
The sun hits the wall
Tears slice my cheek
And I settle in
For the last season of Forever

While the tides of morning
Flood into my weary old house
And a dust-devil dances
In the kitchen window…

Backing Up Today

In a corner of the flash drive's eye
Save enough space for kisses
To store first light
On a sleeping haunch
Follow a tired hand
As it soothes your pillow
Hold the undeletable gratitude
Of pre-dawn breaths

Make it your menu
To speak the unspoken
Write-protect every love note
Label that file
MUST ALWAYS REMEMBER
(Though you know you won't)

Save a place in line
For apropos
Cherish the data
That the body retrieves
The scalp absorbs
And the cowlick remembers.

Leave it unprocessed.

Fold the umbrella
Close the drawer
Spend it now
So it can never cash-out
No task can exhaust it
No greed fragment it
It needs no lock
No flag on the desktop.

Inexhaustible it is
As darkness and silence
It trumps all your tantrums
Blurs your bad habits
Trashes hesitation
Rebuilds your lungs.
So, in muted celebration,

Gift it:
Maybe with romance
Surely with passion
And for the sake of staying,
Perseverance.
Oh yes…

But especially,
    and above all,
Kindness.

Step Away from the House

Step away from the house
And the sky opens up
The stars leap down
Inhaling your itches

Step away from your stories
And the evergreens hum
The wind chases down
Today's cringing evasions

Step away from my hand
And the horizon pinches
Harder than an egg

Step into the night
And a light is burrowing
Beyond your reach
Further than fears

The treetops are a wave-edge
You're over your head.

Look back at the house.
Is that your happiness?
Can those languid children
Lapped in light
Really be your bank?

Too easy.

From behind the house
In the shadows of the gravel
Why isn't something lurking
To spoil it all…
Why is everything
Suddenly so right?

It will pass.

Sweet regret will return.
But for now, my son

Step away from the house
Raise your arms to forever
Wave away the mad mornings
When this river sings harmony
And the willows are waving
Fake blessings at the moon.

Mike Rows On…

He's towing the fog this morning
Drawing it to him,
Brushing away its bedclothes.
Unmuffled oars embrace the river's fizz
So he can wrestle the angels of the harbor
And come away never clear but clearer
Never enlightened but lighter

The restless labor of his lungs
A foghorn gliding out
Wider than his wake
Outdistancing regrets
Overboarding to-do's
Breaking toward the daylight
That refuses to hurry to him
Shaking droplets like a horse
Unwearied by the squint of the salt

Whispering points of no return
Pass him, drown.
He moves
Relentless
Rudderless
Sweeping the horizon,
Lost
Found
Adrift
Foraging

Gazing always skyward
Staying ahead of the planet
As his oars push the globe's shoulders back
Eating the uphill's breakfast
No interest in the downslope

Daring its tides
To turn him around
Earlier than he chooses…

Then gliding.

He opts to exhale
A long one
And while he holds still
The river can resume
The world rolls on again
Seaward, sightless, past him
And he can think…

"Diving for the Sun" photo by Peter Barton

Startle Reaction

Spooked by joy
Her head cocks
The mane splashes
Fingers smooth the table
Hungering to interrogate
Her tight-lipped belly.

The eyes flash, widen
Mouth hesitates to follow
Then slips on a riverbank
Where the current takes her chin down.

So much sequined pain.
I can't take my eyes away.

Unaccustomed
She wrestles ecstasy
Squints
Derails her eyeliner
Growls at its slobbery cringing
Kicks off her unmade blankets
Bulging beyond horizons.

Can she leapfrog the fates?
Combat is so much easier.
Anguish slips comfortably
Between non-committal sheets.

For just a moment,
She grips the table with both hands.
Her rings click, her songs tighten.

Shadows tap the bar window.
Her neck lets her go.
The street is a sporting event
Full of welcome jostling.

Will these crossroads blossom?
Or just go pretzel.
Morning has shattered
So many promises.

And will the moon rock on?

Winter's impatient radiator
Has already hissed away
Cruel maybe after maybe.

The ice in her drink
Raises a finger
As if to summon a stenographer

But no.

At the ache of evening's apogee
Shoulders recall the clouds
When the surf knocked her down.

She leans away
On the arm of exultation
Still startled
Still tilted
Steadily unsteady
Begging a million whats
Volunteering no whys
Craving the shadows
Down under the pier

A cell phone calls for the check.
Another cries out.
A new ring echoes
In the ghost nursery
Far from her home.

It moves next door
A killer robocall
For certain

In the gathering dusk,
Beyond this half shut
Half-open
Swinging door
Mona Lisa bites her tongue.

Veterans' Benefits

What you can't see you can imagine
What you can't hear can't wound
What's around the corner is out of your league
What's coming can wait
No worry about falling
If you can hardly get up…

A Phone Is Ringing in the Next Room

It knifes through the wall
Hurts to my hair
Because it's not for me.

A cell phone rings
Across the world
My daughter is answering
Her ticket's punched
She's coming home
With quick stopovers
In another life
Stomping sour grapes

The building's silent now
Dark descends
Stronger than snow
Merciless
Stifling

A phone is ringing
In the ghost nursery
It moves next door
I want to answer it
But I fear it's for me

My own cell crouches here
Nested, incontinent,
I stroke its spine
And put it to sleep.

Bruises

Love slapped her around 'til her kisses bled
She ran and ran but her hopes ached
She tacked her beauty above the tree line
Popped her faded promises in a cold oven

No timer rang
No fax clawed the counter
Her phone held its breath
Its digits choked to death
She cleaned and washed
'Til the shower screamed

On her knees on the floor
She couldn't find any scraps
Of ecstasy or expectation,
                      giggles or sighs…

Still…
 She neatened her memories
Packed a bag splitting
With unreceived Thank You´s
For undelivered parties

Then
She closed the curtains on Sunday
Declared her independence
And marched out boldly…

To
        her bed
Where she dreamt that her cat
Could be an allergenic weapon
Reopened the curtain
Poked her pillow in the eye
And watched the day dilute
Against the neighbor's tired wall
While her throat filled
With the dusk-breath of bare cupboards
The boxes in the hall
The emptiness of the sink
And the silence of the street…

He Had Always Lived a Laptop Life

Recharging before The Body awakened
At those peasant-blouse one-night stands
Husbanding enough hard disk space
For a half-life of half lies
Wi-fi his wayward hottie
A wandering Aaron more than Moses
A voice of unreason
Projecting way past
Even the farthest boarding gate

The sunrise owned him
Promising a reformat
But by 5 he'd turned his back
On the hiss of unreturned calls
Didn't bother to hit 'save'
Let the day's forgettable produce
Slipperily nod
Into moldy sleep

The sixties were to blame,
Mostly
It took so long to change the world
He grew grumpier than an unhanded child
California mornings were an improvement
Gray on gray bleeding into uncertain afternoons
Maybe a Santa Ana wind after lunch
Drier than his Stoli martini

What's wrong with everybody?
Where did the subjunctive go?
Why is the future shrinking
Eye contact scarcer than hugs
Portfolios oozing
The delayed-exploding venom
Of second and third guesses

Where did the flower children
All dandelion to?
And why can't he remember
His address in '92

When the campus was an ice floe
And he was the only one
Who didn't scramble for shelter?

There Is Coming to You and Going Away

There is the speeding up
When I'm about to see you
And the tide that pulls me away.

Past and future you.

In between is the moment
When your pull turns
Like passing a canoe's glide
From one guiding hand to another
And past and future loving
Are right there
On the cusp
For all to feel
A breath off the lake on the skin…

"Reaching For Sky" photo by Peter Barton at Jacob's Pillow Dance Festival

Days of Holding On

Some days you drive through
Some you wade
Some mornings you shave your face
Some, you try to reshape it
One day, the leaves dance in the wind
The next, they're rotting in the yard…

Is that all?
It's all.
Is there anything more important?
Is there anything more fleeting?

Why do you age me with every sigh,
Every round-the-shoulder glance in my direction?
Why is everything aching when you're near
And everything aching when you go away?

I wait by your morning door
Watching the sun eat up the rug
But you won't come out and play.

I'm not good for much except loving you
What do I do
If you go away?

What's the use of coffee
If it's not in your cup?
What good is a window
If it doesn't light your bed?

I don't want more useless sunsets
And teasing dawns.
I just want you with me
When the afternoons
Turn ugly.

You are an invisible cat around my neck
A song I hum on the road beyond dark
An ingenious way of folding my sweaty pillow
A breath through the window
From lonely trees.

Why do I flock to hug you
And laugh that there's so little of you?
When I've spent so many dreams
Marveling at your hugeness
And so many sun-ups
Holding my breath in the face of
Your rippleless intensity.

Why must you grow stronger
As I grow older?
Why must you go on and on
Yanking back curtains
While I roll over and yearn to breathe in
A dawn wind or two.

Hawks recycle.
I don't.

Come let me take your hand
Until the dusk locks down
The ribs of yesterday
And moves on…

Blessed Are the Joys

Blessed are the joys of remembering a name
It's catching a dish that's falling off of a shelf
Fishing a prize earring out of the toilet
Or saving a baby wandering too close to the surf

Now there goes that song again
I have it, I know it
Google does too

I'll stick an arthritic finger
In the dike of my imagination
And pray that the wind
Carries the I-can't-quite-name-it
Music far away….

We'll Go on One Ticket

We'll go on one ticket
I can't travel alone
I'll pack you a lunch
Our kids liked my menus
I'll bring crosswords
And the dictionary in my head
I'll bring photos
Of you curled up in my hand

I'll flush my regrets
Stale bread upon the waters
I won't look back
Like Orpheus and Dylan
Since you'll be clutching
My mournful hand
And as the day parts
Our symphony will tune up
Waxing their bows
To poke holes in the dawn…

I Will Keep House for You

I will keep house for you
Wherever you may have gone
It's the least I can undo
And I know the least is most
Of what I've been able to do for you.

You will talk to me from the other room
The way you always have
And I'll pretend to hear
Instead of keeping silent
The way I always haven't

I'll keep the oversupply
Of lamps you've loved
Always lit,
Illuminating
empty corners
Their shades a bit burnt
From over-use
And the feckless pillows
You loved to buy
Sitting up soft at attention
In all your old nests.

The sky will lighten
The rains turn to dusk
And still I will keep house
Washing what's not dirty
Tidying where no one looks
Knowing you will no longer follow me
Redoing what I have underdone.

And when the morning paper
Hits the door
The radiators hiss
And the drainpipes sigh
I will wake the house for you
Wrestle the crossword for you
Watch the birds crash
And the planes soar

While New Jersey prevails
And the daffodils droop
And bare branches quiver
Long before dark…

She Waits Patiently for Me

She waits patiently for me
At the edge of the wood
This tree that I've been painting.
I've let the shadows grow
Because removed from her thicket
She'd not be so interesting.
A mongrel kind of tree
With a skin condition
But she understands my mood
And how I think
At this unHappy Hour
Only of a drink
So she gets my mind off it
With a well-barked inbreath
And sometimes shakes her branches
If I make a move to turn around
Home.

Peter **Barton** is an award-winning poet, filmmaker, photographer and author. His poetry explores aging, family, legacy, heartbreak. While serving in the Peace Corps in Chile, Barton began writing poems in response to the Vietnam War. He created a collection of poems as a form of anti-war activism, five of which were published in *The Saturday Review* in 1969.

Barton's poetry won the 2021 2nd and 3rd place cash award at the Westmoreland Arts and Heritage Festival which also published his work. In addition, his poems have been published by the Orchard Street Press.

Dial Press published his book, *Staying Power*, a collection of non-fiction behind- the-scenes profiles of un-rich, un-famous actors, musicians, and dancers—the foot soldiers in the performing arts. Barton's aim was to show young readers that they could find fulfillment on stage without becoming celebrities.

Barton's film work has been featured on CBS, PBS, Showtime, and HBO. Barton has three Emmy nominations and has won three CINE Gold Eagle Awards for his filmmaking. *Riff' 65*, a student film he collaborated on, won the equivalent of a Student Academy Award before the category was officially established.

He began his career teaching at NYU with Marty Scorsese (Oliver Stone was his student), working on the crew of the original *Woodstock* and making politically engaged films with Newsreel. Two films he collaborated on, *Eddie and Janie's Janie*, are in the permanent collection of the Museum of Modern Art.

Barton is the founder of Groundswell, Inc., a non-profit organization dedicated to making documentaries that amplify marginalized voices. Groundswell's film, *Cries from Nagasaki*, an improvised experimental short inspired by children's accounts of the first atomic bombings, was an official selection of the Cannes Shorts Corner, Sedona, Newport, LA and Hollywood DV Film Festivals. His work producing and directing *Names Can Really Hurt Us*, A CBS Anti-Defamation League special, earned him a nomination for the Edward R. Murrow Award and three Emmy nominations. Barton's improvisational feature Film, *The Suicide Auditions*, shot at Niagara Falls, won first prize at the Georgetown Film Festival

He directed, edited, shot and co-produced, *Women of '69, Unboxed*, a portrait of a group of women who graduated from college with high hopes the same year as Hillary Clinton. The film won first prize at the Queens World and New York Indie Festivals, as well as a special audience prize at the Woods Hole Festival. The film was broadcast continent-wide on PBS.

Barton taught film production and screenwriting at New York University, Bennington College, Columbia University and Brooklyn College. He was class poet at Dartmouth where a play he wrote, *Pand*, helped inaugurate the experimental theater at the new Hopkins Center.

He holds an M.F.A. in playwriting and directing from the Yale School of Drama. While there, he wrote and acted in *Dawn Song*, a full-length play about Chief Joseph and the Nez Perce tribe. It inaugurated the Morse College dramat at Yale. On the heels of the Kennedy assassination, the play examined the importance of wise leadership in making lasting change.

His films are currently available on the Groundswell Media Channel on YouTube and on the Groundswell Media website.

www.ingramcontent.com/pod-product-compliance
Lightning Source LLC
Chambersburg PA
CBHW031818110426
42743CB00057B/987